I HATE MY JOB

COLORING BOOK

Enjoying this book?

Please leave a review because we would love to know your thoughts, feedback, and opinions to create better paper products for you!

Thank you so much for your support.

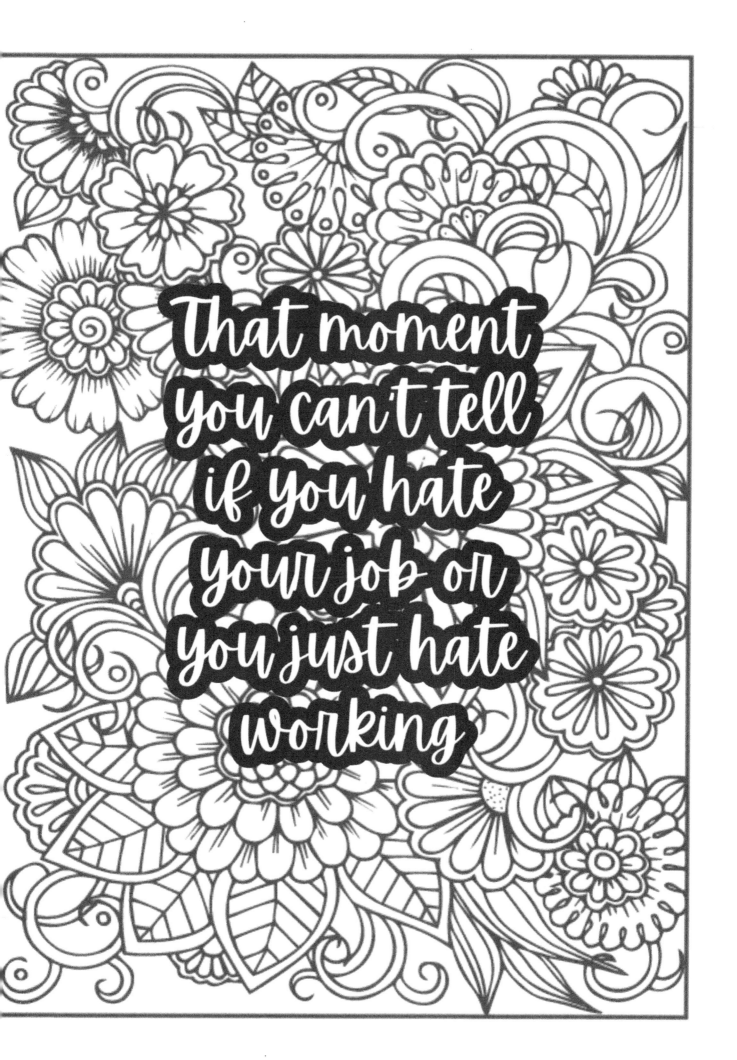

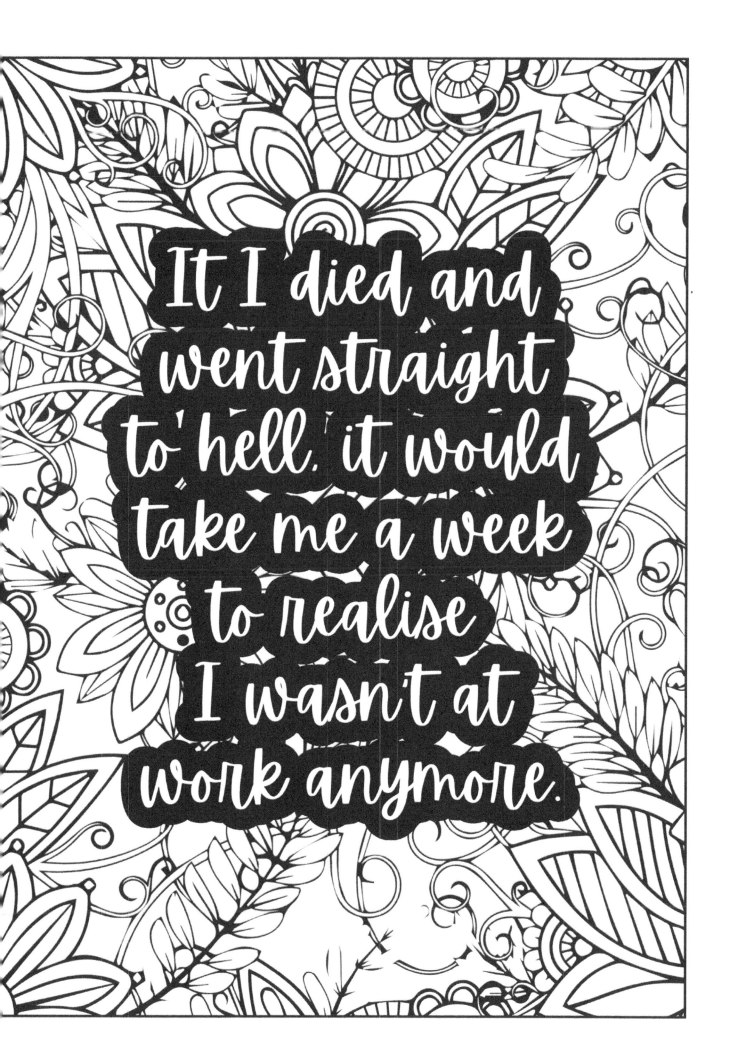

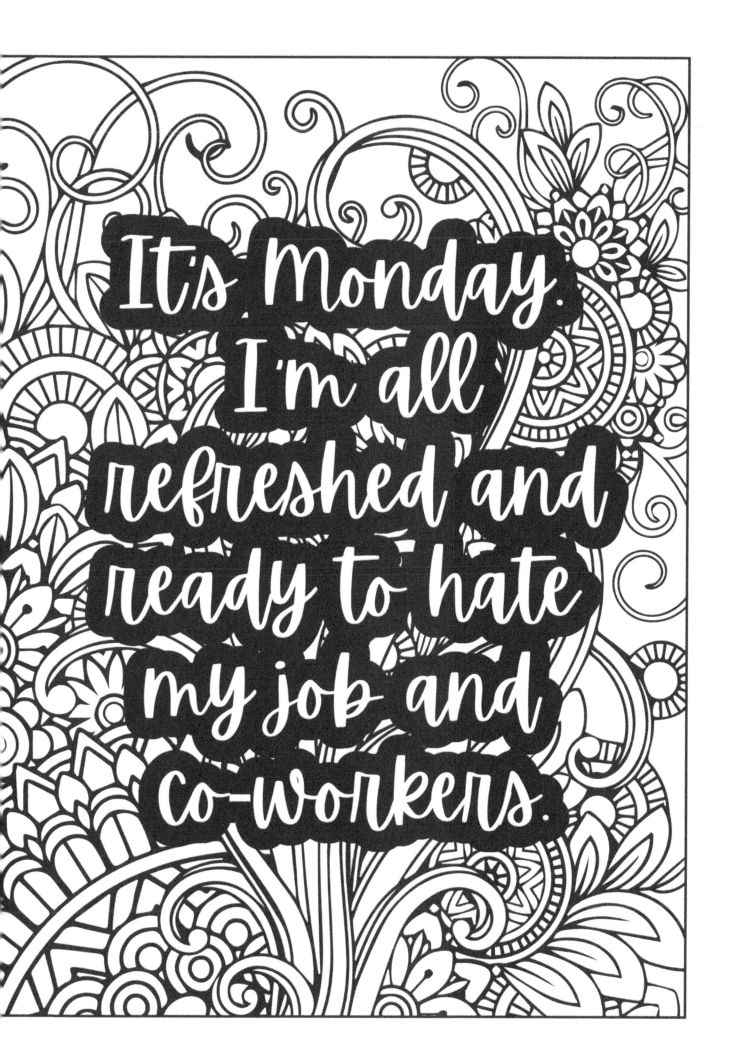

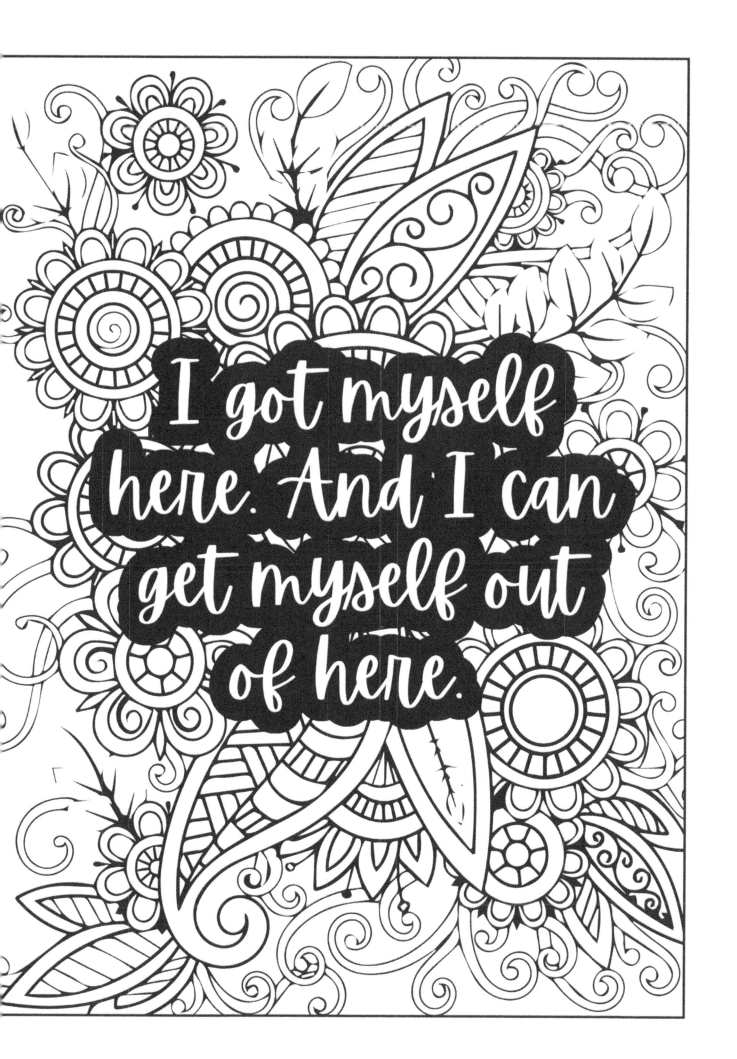

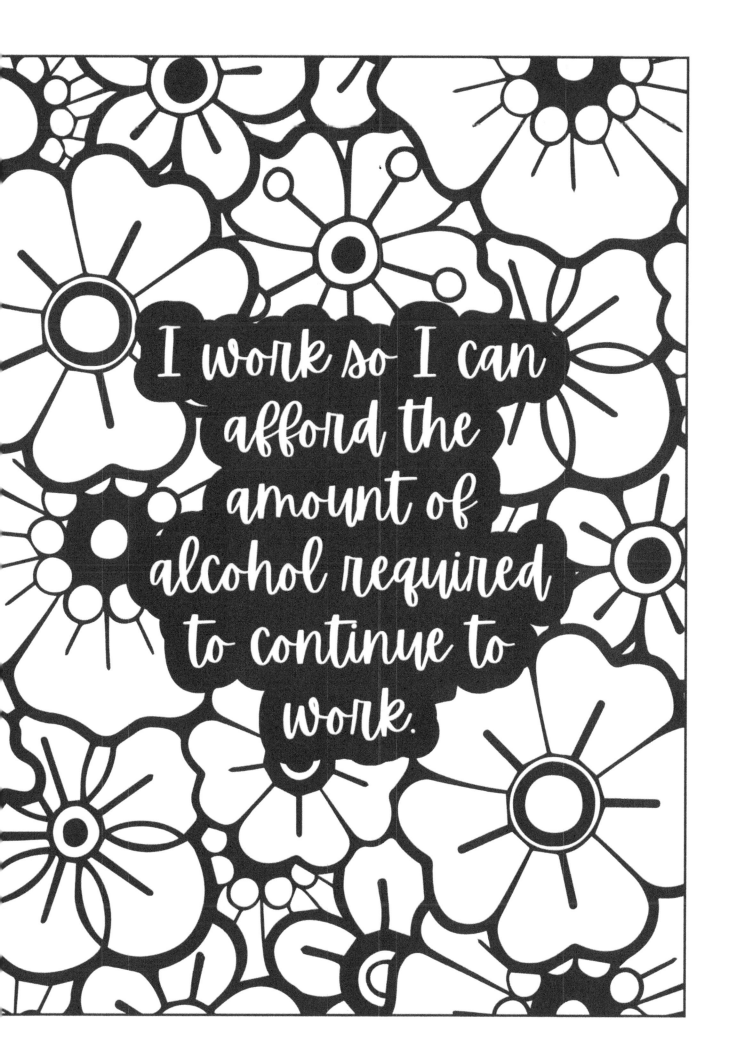

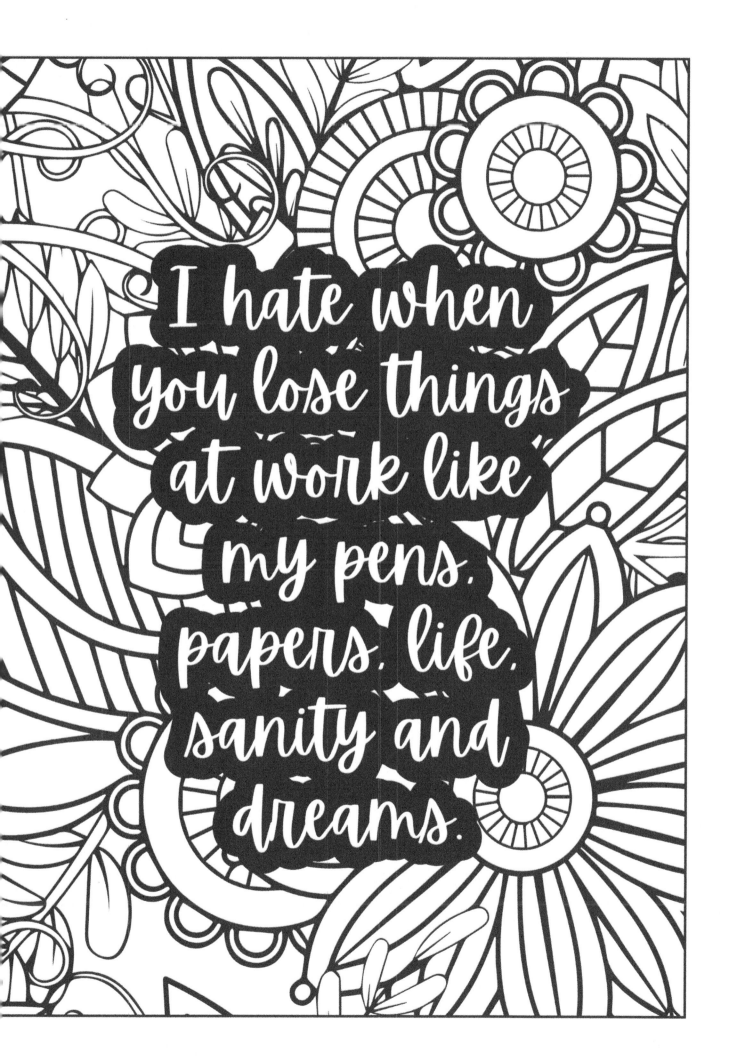

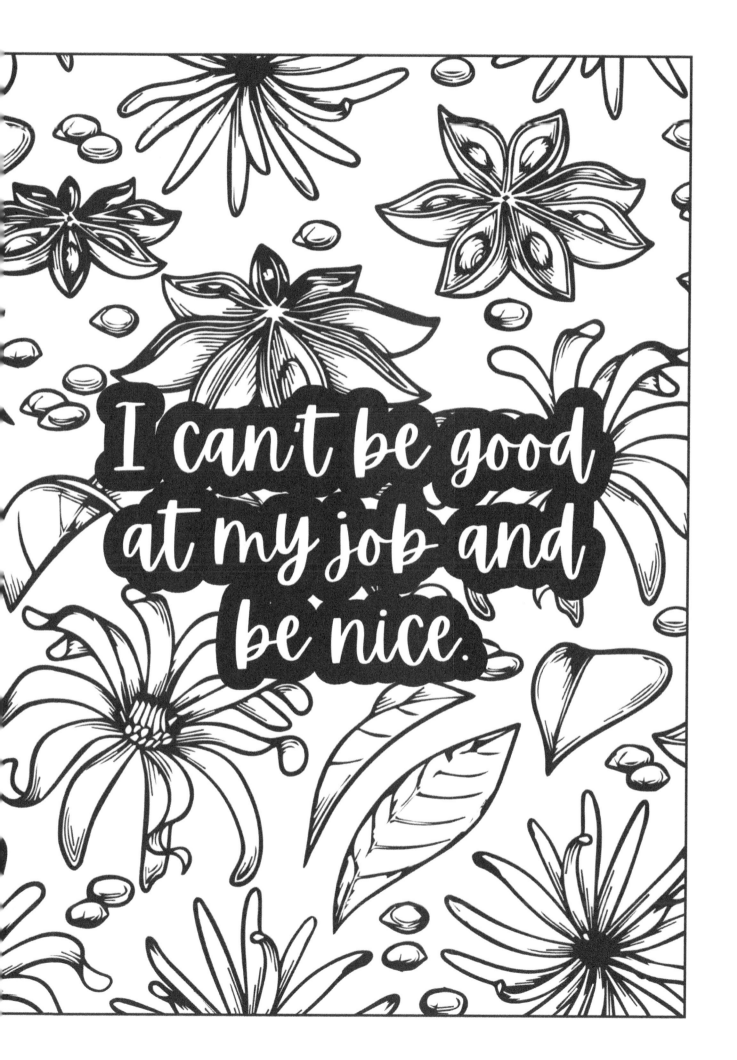

I can't be good at my job and be nice.

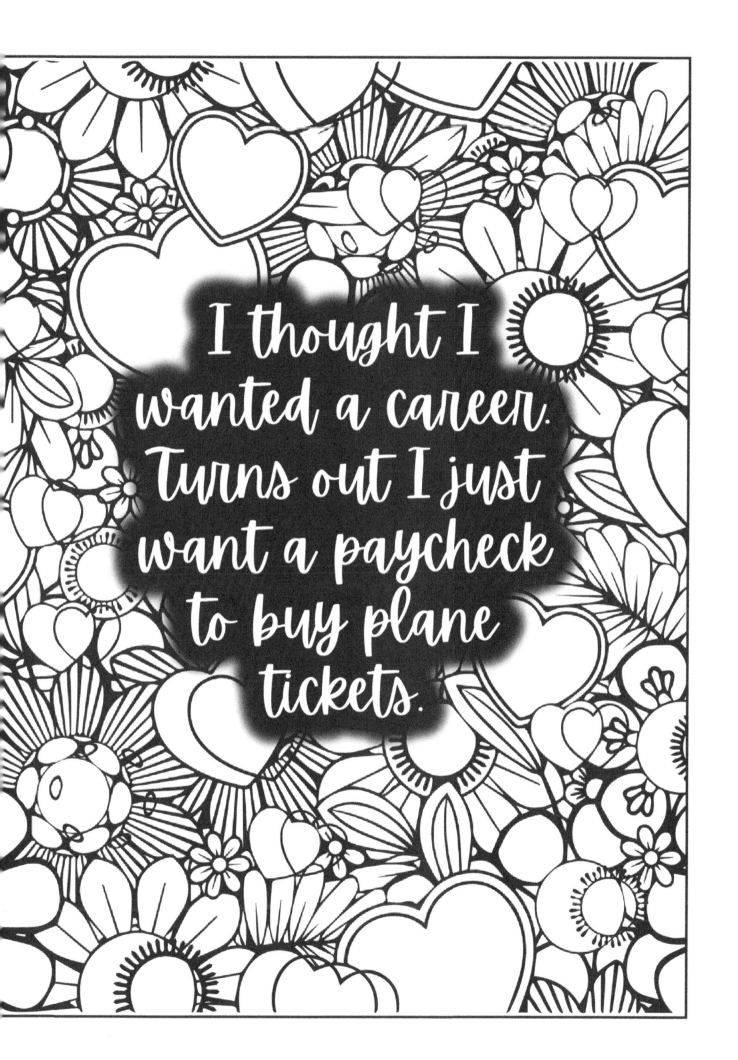

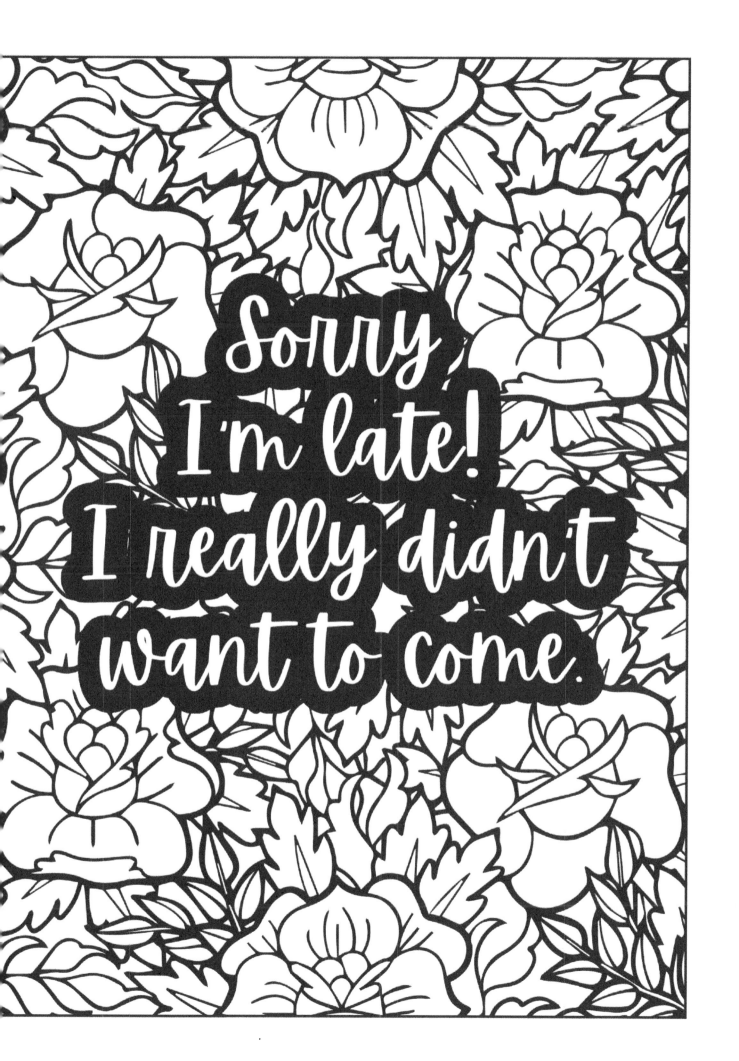

Work tip:
Stand up.
Stretch.
Take a walk.
Go to the airport.
Get on a plane.
Never return.

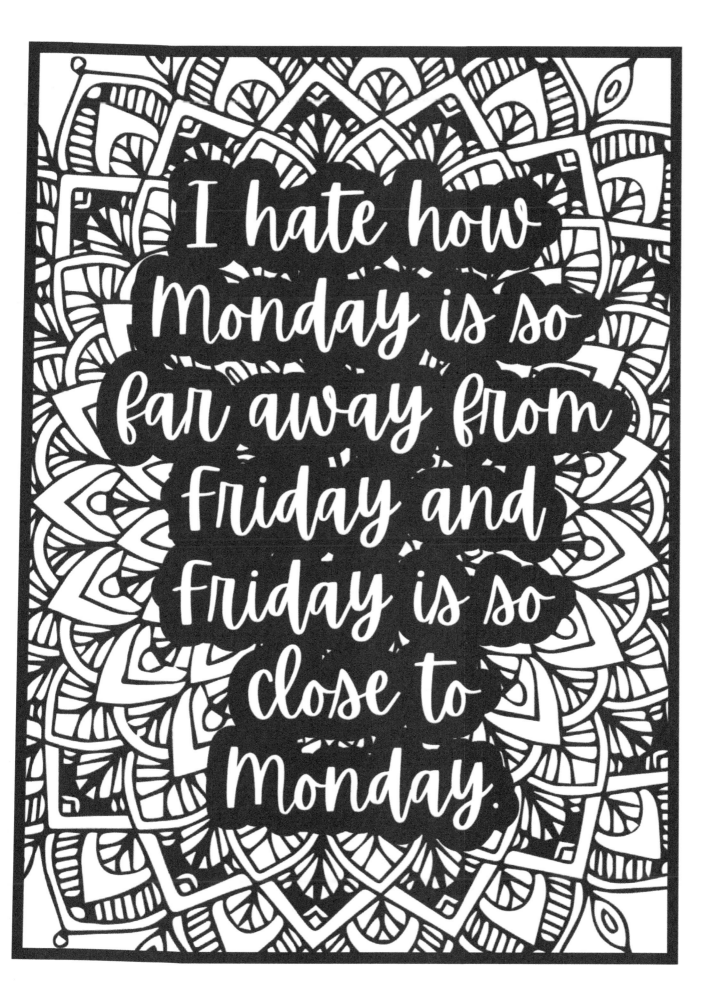

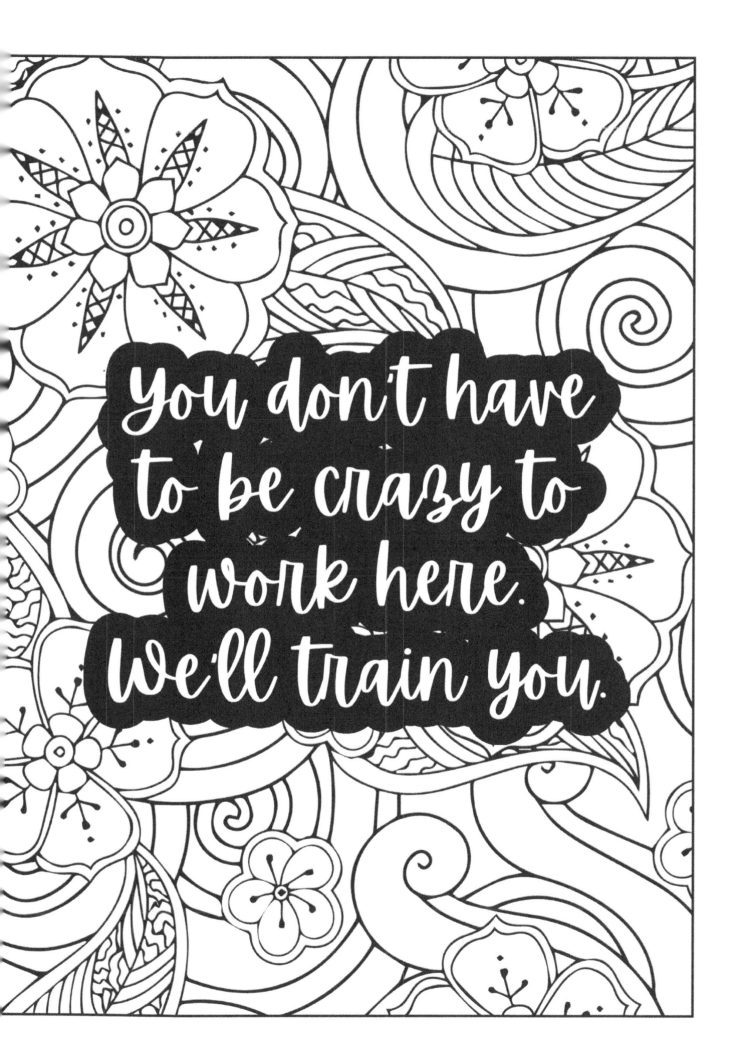

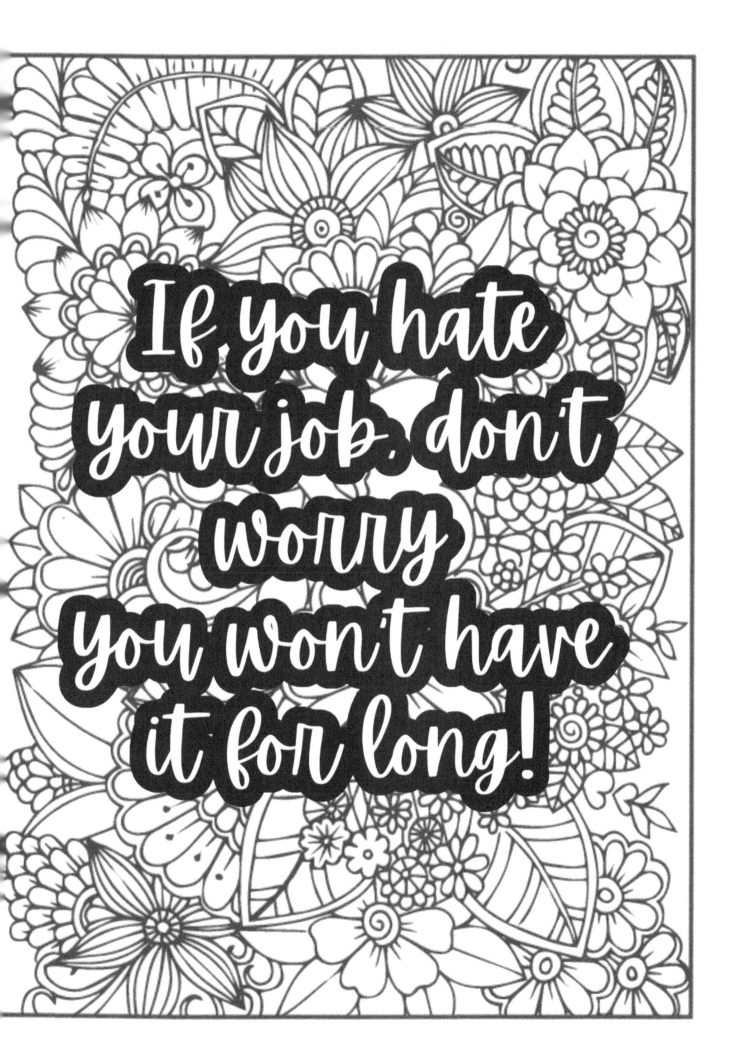

If you hate your job, don't worry you won't have it for long!

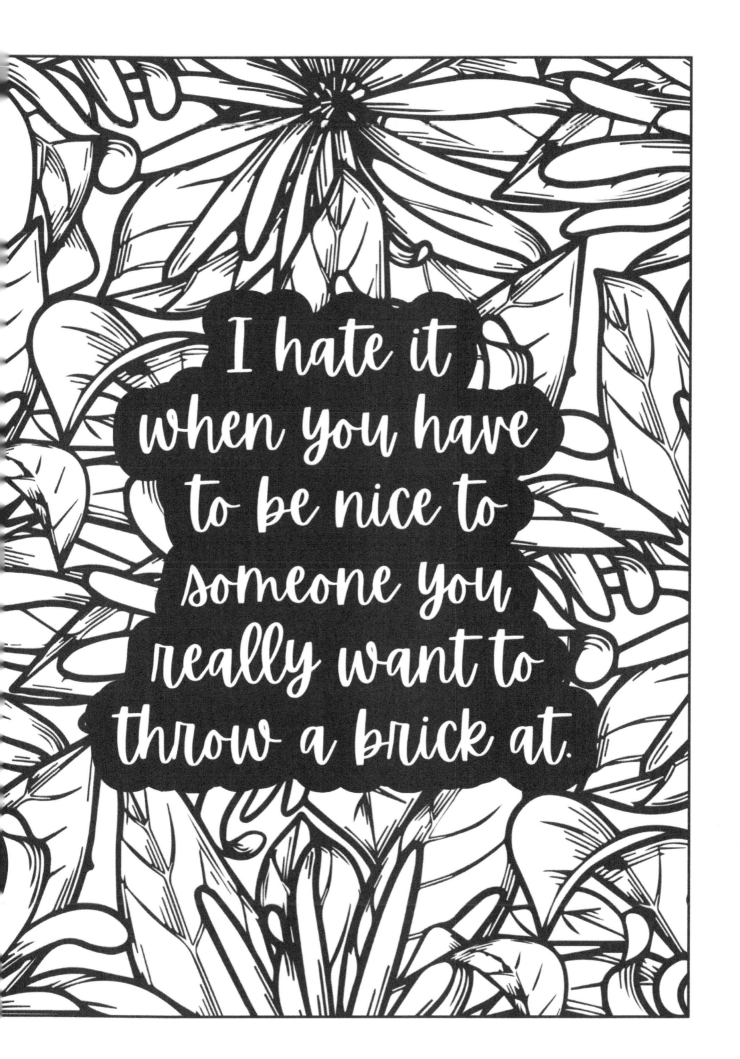

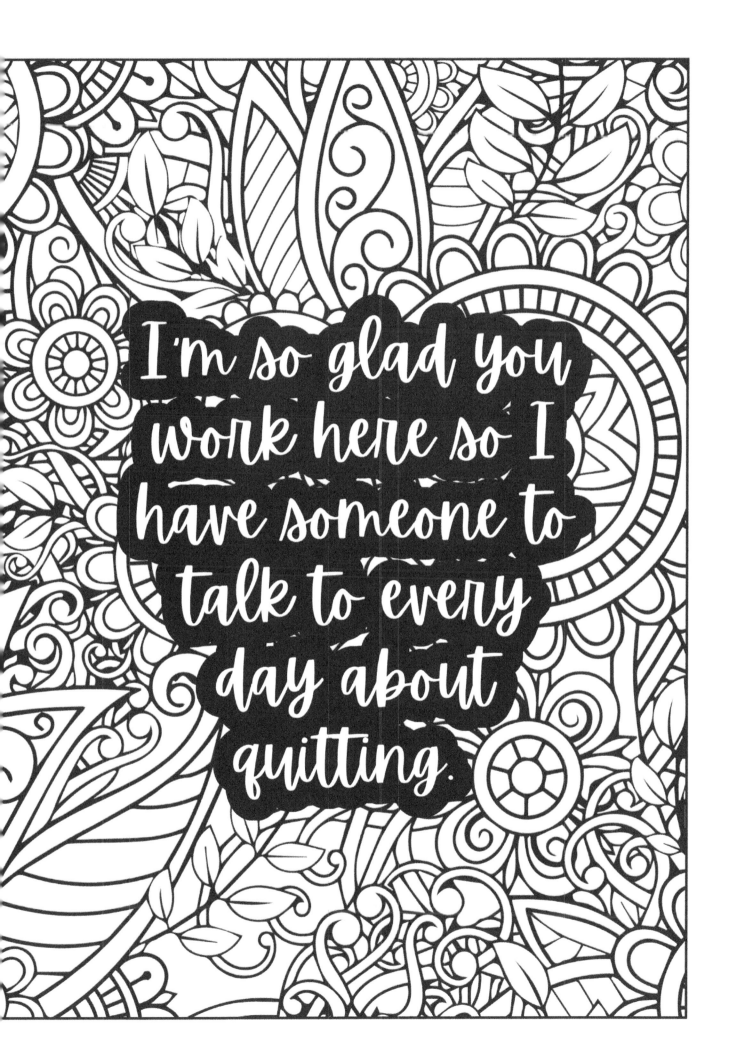

I'm so glad you work here so I have someone to talk to every day about quitting.

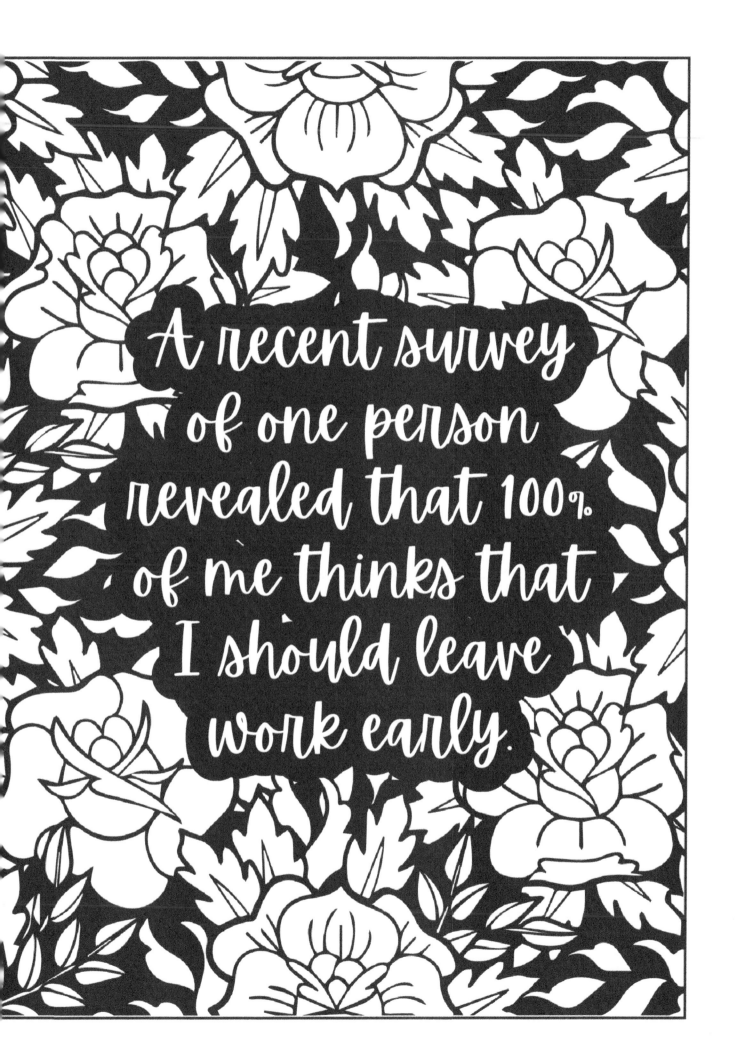

Made in the USA
Las Vegas, NV
12 August 2024

93737459R00031